1

兒童
華語課本

CHILDREN'S
CHINESE READER

中英文版

Chinese-English
Edition

OVERSEAS CHINESE AFFAIRS COMMISSION
中華民國僑務委員會印行

序言

　　我國僑胞遍佈全球，爲加強服務僑胞，傳揚中華文化，推動華語文教學，本會特邀集華語文學者專家於民國八十二年編製這套「兒童華語課本」教材，並深受各界肯定。近年來，採用本教材之僑校持續增加，爲使這套教材更適合海外需求，本會將繼續了解並彙整僑校教師意見，以供未來編修之用。

　　本教材共計十二冊，適於小學一至六年級程度學生使用。每冊四課，以循序漸進的方式編排，不但涵蓋一般問候語到日常生活所需詞彙，並將家庭、學校與人際互動等主題引入課文中。從第七冊起，更加入短文、民俗節慶、寓言及成語故事，使學生在學習華語文的同時，也能對中華文化有所體認。

　　爲讓學生充分了解並運用所學語言及文字，編輯小組特別逐冊逐課編寫作業簿，以看圖填字、文句翻譯、問答等方式提供學生多元化練習的機會，進而加強學生的語文能力。

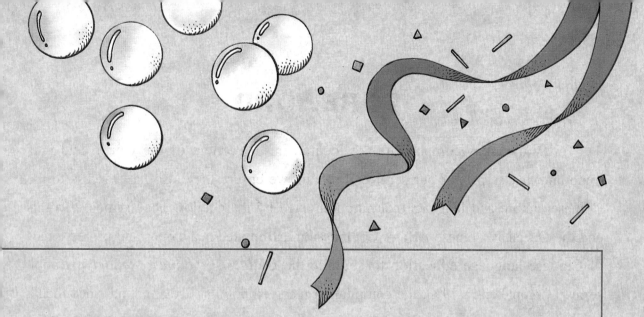

　　海外華文教材推廣的動力在華文教師，是以在課本、作業簿之外，本套教材另提供教學指引及電化教材，教師可靈活運用其中之各項資料，以加強教學效果，提昇學習興趣。

　　語言的精進，端賴持續不斷練習，然而海外學習華語文的環境卻有其時間及空間的限制，必須教師、家長與學生三方密切合作，方能克竟其功。我們希望教師能善用本套材之相關教學資源，提供生動活潑的學習環境，學生家長能參與課後各項輔導活動，讓學生在生活化及自然化的情境中學習，以突破學習的困境。

　　本套教材之編製工作繁複，我們要特別感謝熱心參與的專家學者，由於他們精心地規劃與認真地編寫，使本教材得以順利出版。僑教工作的推展，非一蹴可幾，本會今後將積極結合海內外專家學者及僑教人士，共同為改良華語文教材、提昇華語文教學水準而努力，使僑教工作更為深化扎實。

僑務委員會委員長

張　富　美

FOREWORD

Today overseas compatriots are located in all corners of the world, and it is important that as part of our services to them, we ensure they also have access to the Chinese culture and language education enjoyed by their fellow countrymen. To this end the Overseas Chinese Affairs Commission had invited academics and professionals of Chinese language education to compile the *Children's Chinese Reader* textbook series. Completed in 1993, the compilation received popular acclaim, and since then a continuously increasing number of overseas Chinese schools have based their teaching upon this series. In order to make *Children's Chinese Reader* even better adapted to the needs of overseas teachers and students, the OCAC welcomes the comments and feedback of teachers at overseas Chinese schools for future revisions.

Children's Chinese Reader consists of 12 books and is suitable for primary students from grades 1 to 6. Each book contains 4 step-by-step lessons in increasing levels of difficulty, which not only cover general greetings and vocabulary commonly used in daily life, but also incorporate such themes as family, school and social interactions. Starting from book 7 the lessons introduce short stories, folk celebrations, traditional fables and proverb stories, so that students of the Chinese language may also gain an understanding of Chinese culture.

In order to help students fully comprehend and utilize the vocabulary and knowledge acquired, editors of *Children's Chinese Reader* have designed workbooks that correspond to each textbook in the series. Through fill-in-the-blank questions, sentence translations, and Q and A formats, these workbooks offer students the opportunity to practice in a number of different ways, so as to further enhance their language skills.

Teachers of the Chinese language are the main driving force behind overseas Chinese education. Therefore, in addition to textbooks and workbooks, *Children's Chinese Reader* also offers teaching guidelines and electronic materials that teachers may flexibly adapt as necessary. With these supplementary materials, it is hoped that teachers will be able to inspire the interest of students and achieve their educational goals.

Consistent practice is the key for progress in learning any new language, but students learning the Chinese language overseas are often hampered in their learning environment in terms of time and space. Therefore successful studies will depend on the joint efforts of teachers, parents and students. We hope that teachers will be able to make full use of the educational resources offered by *Children's Chinese Reader* to provide students with a lively and fascinating learning environment. If parents of students can also participate in the various extracurricular activities organized by schools, then students will be able to learn through a daily and natural environment that overcomes barriers to learning.

The compilation of *Children's Chinese Reader* has taken the dedicated and tireless efforts of many people. In particular, we must thank those academics and professionals who have willingly given their time and expertise. It was only because of their meticulous planning and painstaking care in drafting that the series successfully came to be published. Propagation of Chinese language education overseas is not a work that can be completed in the short-term. In the future, the OCAC will continue to cooperate with local and overseas professionals and educators in further improving teaching materials for the Chinese language and enhancing the quality of Chinese language education.

Chang Fu-mei, Ph.D.
Minister of Overseas Chinese Affairs Commission

兒童華語課本中英文版編輯要旨

一、本書為中華民國僑務委員會為配合北美地區華裔子弟適應環境需要而編寫，教材全套共計課本十二冊、作業簿十二冊及教師手冊十二冊。另每課製作六十分鐘錄影帶總計四十八輯，提供教學應用。

二、本書編輯小組及審查委員會於中華民國七十七年十一月正式組成，編輯小組於展開工作前擬定三項原則及五項步驟，期能順利達成教學目標：

(一)三項原則——

(1)介紹中國文化與中國人的思維方式，以期海外華裔子弟能了解、欣賞並接納我國文化。

(2)教學目標在表達與溝通，以期華裔子弟能聽、說、讀、寫，實際運用中文。

(3)教材內容大多取自海外華裔子弟當地日常生活，使其對課文內容產生認同感，增加實際練習機會。

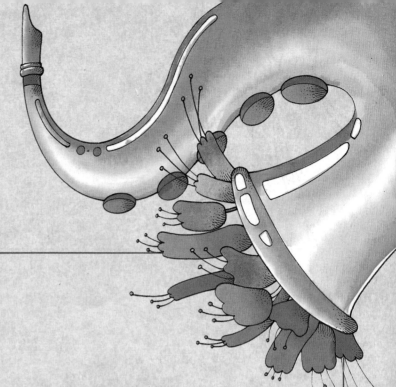

　　㈡五項步驟——

　　　　(1)分析學習者實際需要，進而決定單元內容。

　　　　(2)依據兒童心理發展理論擬定課程大綱：由具體事
　　　　　　物而逐漸進入抽象、假設和評估階段。

　　　　(3)決定字彙、詞彙和句型數量，合理地平均分配於
　　　　　　每一單元。

　　　　(4)按照上述分析與組織著手寫作課文。

　　　　(5)增加照片、插圖、遊戲和活動，期能吸引學童注
　　　　　　意力，在愉快的氣氛下有效率地學習。

三、本書第一至三冊俱採注音符號（ㄅ、ㄆ、ㄇ、ㄈ……）
　　及羅馬拼音。第四冊起完全以注音符號與漢字對照為
　　主。

四、本書適用對象包括以下三類學童：

　　㈠自第一冊開始——在北美洲土生土長、無任何華語
　　　基礎與能力者。

　　㈡自第二冊開始——因家庭影響，能聽說華語，卻不

　　識漢字者。

　　㈢自第五或第六冊開始——自國內移民至北美洲，稍
　　　具國內基本國語文教育素養；或曾於海外華文學校
　　　短期就讀，但識漢字不滿三百字者。

五、本書於初級華語階段，完全以注音符號第一式及第二
　　式介紹日常對話及句型練習，進入第三冊後，乃以海
　　外常用字作有計劃而漸進之逐字介紹，取消注音符號
　　第二式，並反覆練習。全書十二冊共介紹漢字 1160
　　個，字彙、詞彙共 1536 個，句型 217 個，足供海外
　　華裔子弟閱讀一般書信、報紙及書寫表達之用。並在
　　第十一冊、十二冊增編中國四大節日及風俗習慣作閱
　　讀的練習與參考。

六、本書教學方式採溝通式教學法，著重於日常生活中的
　　表達與溝通和師生間之互動練習。因此第一至七冊完
　　全以對話形態出現；第八冊開始有「自我介紹」、
　　「日記」、「書信」和「故事」等單元，以學生個人

生活經驗為題材，極為實用。

七、本書每一主題深淺度也配合著兒童心理之發展，初級
課程以具象實物為主，依語文程度和認知心理之發展
逐漸添加抽象思考之概念，以提升學生自然掌握華語
文實用能力。初級課程之生字與對話是以口語化的發
音為原則，有些字需唸輕聲，語調才能自然。

八、本書編輯旨意，乃在訓練異鄉成長的中華兒女，多少
能接受我中華文化之薰陶，毋忘根本，對祖國語言文
化維繫著一份血濃於水的情感。

九、本書含教科書、作業簿及教師手冊之編輯小組成員為
何景賢博士，宋靜如女士，及王孫元平女士，又經美
國及加拿大地區僑校教師多人及夏威夷大學賀上賢教
授參與提供意見，李芊小姐、文惠萍小姐校對，始克
完成。初版如有疏漏之處，尚祈教師與學生家長不吝
惠正。

Learning Chinese in the English Speaking Environment The Comparison between a Phonetic Symbol System and A Romanization System

Whether a Phonetic Symbol system or a Romanization System is a better way to learn Chinese in an English environment is still a controversial issue. The editors of this book suggest that children learn Phonetic Symbols from primary school onward so that they may get great benefits from it early. Their suggestion is based on the following points:

1. The difference between a Romanization System and the alphabet may cause recognition interference to the primary school children, especially the first and second graders. However, there is no interference if they learn Phonetic Symbols.

2. Critics complain that the 37 Phonetic Symbols are hard to memorize, while it is easier to learn the 26 letters of English alphabet. Actually , the fundamental goal of learning Chinese is to recognize and read Chinese characters, not just stay at the level of learning Phonetic Symbols or Romanization Systems. The Phonetic Symbols derived from the stroke of Chinese characters will be conducive to children in learning Chinese characters. Compared with the Phonetic Symbols, the Romanization Systems do not provide this advantage.

3. Many reading materials for children are written in traditional Chinese characters with the Phonetic Symbols inscribed on the side of the texts. This may enhance the children's Chinese language proficiency. The previous statement is based on 80 (or more) years of experiences in Chinese language teaching, from mainland China to Taiwan and other areas.

To teach children the Phonetic Symbols to learn Chinese does not mean to exclude learning a Romanization System. They can use the System from junior high onward, especially for keying in on PCs. They will find that a Romanization System works well.

目錄
Contents

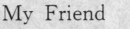

注音符號第一、二式與通用、漢語拼音對照表

注音符號第一式		注音符號第二式	通用拼音	漢語拼音
（一）聲母				
脣音	ㄅㄆㄇㄈ	b p m f	b p m f	b p m f
舌尖音	ㄉㄊㄋㄌ	d t n l	d t n l	d t n l
舌根音	ㄍㄎㄏ	g k h	g k h	g k h
舌面音	ㄐㄑㄒ	j(i) ch(i) sh(i)	ji ci si	j(i) q(i) x(i)
翹舌音	ㄓㄔㄕㄖ	j(r) ch(r) sh(r) r	jh ch sh r	zh ch sh r
舌齒音	ㄗㄘㄙ	tz ts(z) s(z)	z c s	z c s
（二）韻母				
單韻	一ㄨㄩ	(y)i , u,w iu,yu	(y)i , wu,u yu	i u ü
單韻	ㄚㄛㄜㄝ	a o e e	a o e ê	a o e ê
複韻	ㄞㄟㄠㄡ	ai ei au ou	ai ei ao ou	ai ei ao ou
隨聲韻	ㄢㄣㄤㄥ	an en ang eng	an en ang eng	an en ang eng
捲舌韻	ㄦ	er	er	er

第一課

早

Good Morning !

I 對　話

（ Dialogue ）

第　一　部	Part 1
王　芸	早！
李　立	你早！你叫什麼名字？
王　芸	我姓王，名字叫芸。
李　立	喔！王芸。你好，我叫李立。
王　芸	你好！李立。
李　立	老師早！
老　師	你早！
李　立	老師您貴姓？
老　師	我姓林。

李立		您是林老師。
老師		對了！你叫什麼名字？
李立		我叫李立。
王芸		伯伯，您早！
張伯伯		你早！
王芸		請問您貴姓？
張伯伯		我姓張。
王芸		張伯伯。
張伯伯		你叫什麼名字？
王芸		我叫王芸。

3

Ⅰ 對　話

（ Dialogue ）

(Ding Ling！The bell rings.)

王ㄨㄤˊ　芸ㄩㄣˊ　　張ㄓㄤ伯ㄅㄛˊ伯ㄅㄛ˙再ㄗㄞˋ見ㄐㄧㄢˋ！

張ㄓㄤ伯ㄅㄛˊ伯ㄅㄛ˙　再ㄗㄞˋ見ㄐㄧㄢˋ！王ㄨㄤˊ芸ㄩㄣˊ。

II 生字生詞

（Vocabulary & Expressions）

1. 早 ㄗㄠˇ tzǎu Good morning！

2. 你 ㄋㄧˇ nǐ you（singular）

3. 叫 ㄐㄧㄠˋ jiàu my name is... I'm...

4. 什 ㄕㄜˊ 麼 ㄇㄜ shémme what

5. 名 ㄇㄧㄥˊ 字 ㄗˋ（ㄗ）míngtz name

6. 我 ㄨㄛˇ wǒ I, me

7. 姓 ㄒㄧㄥˋ shìng family name, last name

8. 王 ㄨㄤˊ Wáng （a person's family name）

9. 芸 ㄩㄣˊ Yún （a person's given name）

10. 喔 ㄛˋ òu （exclamation）Oh!

11. 你 ㄋㄧˇ 好 ㄏㄠˇ nǐ hǎu How are you？

12. 李 ㄌㄧˇ Lǐ （a person's family name ; last name）

13. 立 ㄌㄧˋ Lì （a person's given name）

14. 老 ㄌㄠˇ 師 ㄕ lǎushr teacher

15. 您 ㄋㄧㄣˊ nín you ;（showing politeness, respect and honor）

16. 貴 ㄍㄨㄟˋ 姓 ㄒㄧㄥˋ guèi shìng What's your（honorable）family name？

17. 林 ㄌㄧㄣˊ Lín （a person's family name）

Ⅱ 生字生詞

（Vocabulary & Expressions）

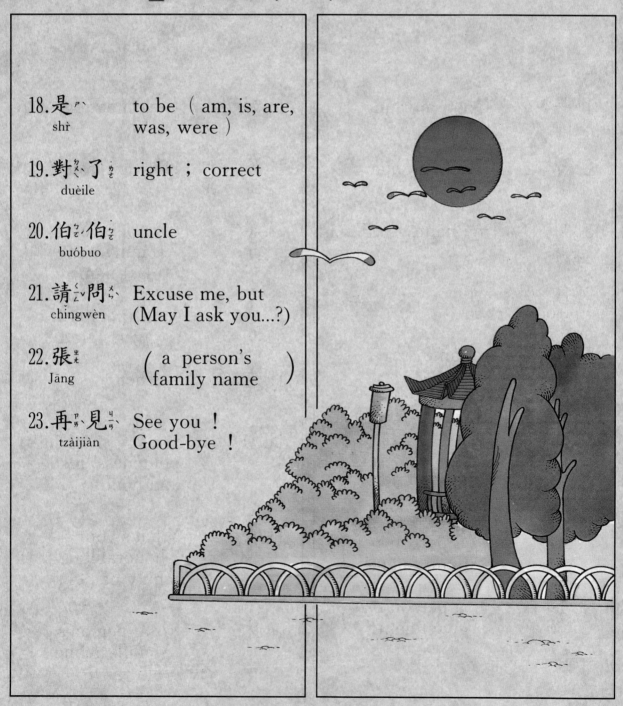

18. 是ㄕˋ　　　to be（am, is, are,
    shì　　　　 was, were）

19. 對ㄉㄨㄟˋ了ㄌㄜ　right；correct
    duèile

20. 伯ㄅㄛˊ伯ㄅㄛ˙　uncle
    buóbuo

21. 請ㄑㄧㄥˇ問ㄨㄣˋ　Excuse me, but
    chǐngwèn　 (May I ask you...?)

22. 張ㄓㄤ　　　（a person's
    Jāng　　　　 family name ）

23. 再ㄗㄞˋ見ㄐㄧㄢˋ　See you！
    tzàijiàn　 Good-bye！

Ⅲ 句型練習

(Pattern Practice)

1.　　　　　　早ㄗㄠˇ

　　　　　您ㄋㄧㄣˊ早ㄗㄠˇ

　　　　老ㄌㄠˇ師ㄕ早ㄗㄠˇ

　　　林ㄌㄧㄣˊ老ㄌㄠˇ師ㄕ早ㄗㄠˇ

　　　張ㄓㄤ老ㄌㄠˇ師ㄕ早ㄗㄠˇ

　　　王ㄨㄤˊ老ㄌㄠˇ師ㄕ早ㄗㄠˇ

　　　李ㄌㄧˇ老ㄌㄠˇ師ㄕ早ㄗㄠˇ

Ⅲ句型練習

(Pattern Practice)

早ㄗㄠˇ

您ㄋㄧㄣˊ早ㄗㄠˇ

伯ㄅㄛˊ伯ㄅㄛˊ早ㄗㄠˇ

林ㄌㄧㄣˊ伯ㄅㄛˊ伯ㄅㄛˊ早ㄗㄠˇ

張ㄓㄤ伯ㄅㄛˊ伯ㄅㄛˊ早ㄗㄠˇ

王ㄨㄤˊ伯ㄅㄛˊ伯ㄅㄛˊ早ㄗㄠˇ

李ㄌㄧˇ伯ㄅㄛˊ伯ㄅㄛˊ早ㄗㄠˇ

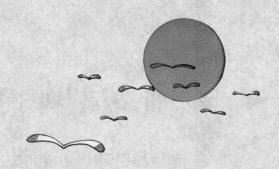

好ㄏㄠˇ

你ㄋㄧˇ好ㄏㄠˇ

您ㄋㄧㄣˊ好ㄏㄠˇ

老ㄌㄠˇ師ㄕ好ㄏㄠˇ

伯ㄅㄛˊ伯ㄅㄛˊ好ㄏㄠˇ

林ㄌㄧㄣˊ老ㄌㄠˇ師ㄕ好ㄏㄠˇ

張ㄓㄤ老ㄌㄠˇ師ㄕ好ㄏㄠˇ

王ㄨㄤˊ老ㄌㄠˇ師ㄕ好ㄏㄠˇ

李ㄌㄧˇ老ㄌㄠˇ師ㄕ好ㄏㄠˇ

林ㄌㄧㄣˊ伯ㄅㄛˊ伯ㄅㄛˊ好ㄏㄠˇ

張ㄓㄤ伯ㄅㄛˊ伯ㄅㄛˊ好ㄏㄠˇ

王ㄨㄤˊ伯ㄅㄛˊ伯ㄅㄛˊ好ㄏㄠˇ

李ㄌㄧˇ伯ㄅㄛˊ伯ㄅㄛˊ好ㄏㄠˇ

Ⅲ 句型練習

（ Pattern Practice ）

2.　你ㄋㄧˇ叫ㄐㄧㄠˋ什ㄕㄜˊ麼ㄇㄜ 名ㄇㄧㄥˊ字ㄗˋ ？　　我ㄨㄛˇ叫ㄐㄧㄠˋ李ㄌㄧˇ立ㄌㄧˋ

　　　　　　　　　　　　　　　　　　我ㄨㄛˇ叫ㄐㄧㄠˋ王ㄨㄤˊ芸ㄩㄣˊ

　　　　　　　　　　　　　　　　　　我ㄨㄛˇ叫ㄐㄧㄠˋ＿＿＿＿＿＿

3.　你ㄋㄧˇ叫ㄐㄧㄠˋ什ㄕㄜˊ麼ㄇㄜ 名ㄇㄧㄥˊ字ㄗˋ ？我ㄨㄛˇ姓ㄒㄧㄥˋ王ㄨㄤˊ，名ㄇㄧㄥˊ字ㄗˋ叫ㄐㄧㄠˋ芸ㄩㄣˊ

　　　　　　　　　　　　　　　　我ㄨㄛˇ姓ㄒㄧㄥˋ李ㄌㄧˇ，名ㄇㄧㄥˊ字ㄗˋ叫ㄐㄧㄠˋ立ㄌㄧˋ

　　　　　　　　　　　　　　　　我ㄨㄛˇ姓ㄒㄧㄥˋ＿＿＿ 名ㄇㄧㄥˊ字ㄗˋ叫ㄐㄧㄠˋ＿＿

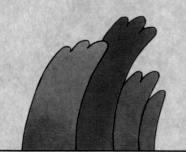

4. 您_{ㄋㄧㄣˊ}貴_{ㄍㄨㄟˋ}姓_{ㄒㄧㄥˋ}？ 　　　　我_{ㄨㄛˇ}姓_{ㄒㄧㄥˋ}林_{ㄌㄧㄣˊ}

　　　　　　　　　　　　　我_{ㄨㄛˇ}姓_{ㄒㄧㄥˋ}王_{ㄨㄤˊ}

　　　　　　　　　　　　　我_{ㄨㄛˇ}姓_{ㄒㄧㄥˋ}張_{ㄓㄤ}

　　　　　　　　　　　　　我_{ㄨㄛˇ}姓_{ㄒㄧㄥˋ}李_{ㄌㄧˇ}

　　　　　　　　　　　　　我_{ㄨㄛˇ}姓_{ㄒㄧㄥˋ}＿＿＿＿＿。

5. 請_{ㄑㄧㄥˇ}問_{ㄨㄣˋ}您_{ㄋㄧㄣˊ}貴_{ㄍㄨㄟˋ}姓_{ㄒㄧㄥˋ}？ 　我_{ㄨㄛˇ}姓_{ㄒㄧㄥˋ}林_{ㄌㄧㄣˊ}

　　　　　　　　　　　　　　　　王_{ㄨㄤˊ}

　　　　　　　　　　　　　　　　張_{ㄓㄤ}

　　　　　　　　　　　　　我_{ㄨㄛˇ}姓_{ㄒㄧㄥˋ}＿＿＿＿＿。

Ⅲ 句型練習

（ Pattern Practice ）

6. 再見！

張伯伯再見！

林老師再見！

＿＿＿＿＿＿＿再見！

IV英 譯

(English Translation)

Part 1：

王ㄨㄤˊ 芸ㄩㄣˊ	Good morning！
李ㄌㄧˇ 立ㄌㄧˋ	Good morning！ What's your name？
王ㄨㄤˊ 芸ㄩㄣˊ	My family name is Wang. My first name is Yun.
李ㄌㄧˇ 立ㄌㄧˋ	Oh！ Wang Yun. Hello！ My name is Li Li.
王ㄨㄤˊ 芸ㄩㄣˊ	Hello, Li Li.
李ㄌㄧˇ 立ㄌㄧˋ	Good morning, Teacher.
老ㄌㄠˇ 師ㄕ	Good morning！

Ⅳ 英 譯

(English Translation)

李立	What's your （ honorable ） family name ?
老師	My family name is Lin.
李立	You are the teacher Mr. Lin.
老師	Right. What's your name ?
李立	My name is Li Li.
王芸	Good morning, Uncle.
張伯伯	Good morning ！
王芸	Excuse me, but may I ask your family name ?

張_{ㄓㄤ}伯_{ㄅㄛ}伯_{ㄅㄛ}	My family name is Jang.
王_{ㄨㄤ} 芸_{ㄩㄣ}	Uncle Jang.
張_{ㄓㄤ}伯_{ㄅㄛ}伯_{ㄅㄛ}	What's your name？
王_{ㄨㄤ} 芸_{ㄩㄣ}	My name is Wang Yun.
	(Ding Ling ！ The bell rings.)
王_{ㄨㄤ} 芸_{ㄩㄣ}	See you, Uncle Jang.
張_{ㄓㄤ}伯_{ㄅㄛ}伯_{ㄅㄛ}	See you, Wang Yun.

第二課

我的家

My Home

16

Ⅰ 對 話

（ Dialogue ）

第 一 部	Part 1
王 芸	爸爸早！媽媽早！
爸 媽	早啊！小芸。
	(Getting dressed and having breakfast)
王 芸	哥哥！快點兒！姐姐，快點兒！
哥 哥	校車來了，對不對？
王 芸	對啊！校車來了！
哥 哥	爸爸再見！
	媽媽再見！

17

I 對 話

（ Dialogue ）

姐姐	爸爸再見！
	媽媽再見！
王芸	爸爸再見！
	媽媽再見！
李立	媽！我回來了！
	爸爸回來了嗎
媽媽	回來了！
李立	妹妹呢？
媽媽	她也回來了。
李立	她在那兒？

媽ㄇㄚ媽˙ㄇㄚ		在ㄗㄞˋ後ㄏㄡˋ院ㄩㄢˋ兒ㄦˊ。
李ㄌㄧˇ立ㄌㄧˋ		弟ㄉㄧˋ弟˙ㄉㄧ在ㄗㄞˋ那ㄋㄞˇ兒ㄦˊ？
媽ㄇㄚ媽˙ㄇㄚ		在ㄗㄞˋ張ㄓㄤ伯ㄅㄛˊ伯˙ㄅㄛ家ㄐㄧㄚ。

19

Ⅱ 生字生詞

(Vocabulary & Expressions)

1. 的˙ㄉㄜ　　　(possessive word)

　　我ㄨㄛˇ的˙ㄉㄜ　my

2. 家ㄐㄧㄚ　　　home

3. 爸ㄅㄚˋ爸˙ㄅㄚ　Dad

4. 媽ㄇㄚ媽˙ㄇㄚ　Mom

5. 啊˙ㄚ　　　　(exclamation) Ah!

6. 小ㄒㄧㄠˇ　　little

7. 哥ㄍㄜ哥˙ㄍㄜ　older brother

8. 姐ㄐㄧㄝˇ姐˙ㄐㄧㄝ　older sister

9. 快ㄎㄨㄞˋ　　Hurry up！

10. 一ㄧˋ點ㄉㄧㄢˇ兒ㄦ（ㄉㄧㄚˇㄦ）a little

11. 校ㄒㄧㄠˋ車ㄔㄜ　school bus

12. 來ㄌㄞˊ　　　come

13. 了˙ㄌㄜ　　　indicating completed action, or changes of state or condition

14. 對ㄉㄨㄟˋ　　yes; right

15. 不ㄅㄨˋ；ㄅㄨˊ；˙ㄅㄨ　no；not,

16. 回來 (ㄏㄨㄟˊ ㄌㄞˊ) come back ;
    return

17. 嗎 (ㄇㄚ) (question word)

18. 妹妹 (ㄇㄟˋ ㄇㄟ) younger sister

19. 呢 (ㄋㄜ) (question word)

20. 她 (ㄊㄚ) she ; her

21. 也 (ㄧㄝˇ) also ; too

22. 在 (ㄗㄞˋ) to be
    (in a location)

23. 那兒 (ㄋㄚˇ ㄦ) where

24. 後院兒 (ㄏㄡˋ ㄩㄢˋ ㄦ) back yard

25. 弟弟 (ㄉㄧˋ ㄉㄧ) younger brother

Ⅲ 句型練習

（ Pattern Practice ）

1.　　　　　　早ㄗㄠˇ？

　　　　　　你ㄋㄧˇ早ㄗㄠˇ？

　　　　　　您ㄋㄧㄣˊ早ㄗㄠˇ？

　　　　　　爸ㄅㄚˋ爸ㄅㄚˋ早ㄗㄠˇ？

　　　　　　媽ㄇㄚ媽ㄇㄚ早ㄗㄠˇ？

　　　　　　哥ㄍㄜ哥ㄍㄜ早ㄗㄠˇ？

　　　　　　姐ㄐㄧㄝˇ姐ㄐㄧㄝ早ㄗㄠˇ？

2.　校ㄒㄧㄠˋ車ㄔㄜ

　　爸ㄅㄚˋ爸ㄅㄚ˙

　　媽ㄇㄚ媽ㄇㄚ˙

　　老ㄌㄠˇ師ㄕ

　　張ㄓㄤ伯ㄅㄛˊ伯ㄅㄛˊ

Ⅲ 句型練習

（Pattern Practice）

3. 我ㄨㄛˇ

她ㄊㄚ

爸ㄅㄚˋ爸ㄅㄚ˙

媽ㄇㄚ媽ㄇㄚ˙

哥ㄍㄜ哥ㄍㄜ˙

姐ㄐㄧㄝˇ姐ㄐㄧㄝ˙

弟ㄉㄧˋ弟ㄉㄧ˙

妹ㄇㄟˋ妹ㄇㄟ˙

回ㄏㄨㄟˊ來ㄌㄞˊ了ㄌㄜ˙

4. 她ㄊㄚ 　　　　　　　　　　回ㄏㄨㄟˊ來ㄌㄞˊ了ㄌㄜ˙嗎ㄇㄚ？

爸ㄅㄚˋ爸ㄅㄚˋ

媽ㄇㄚ媽ㄇㄚ

林ㄌㄧㄣˊ老ㄌㄠˇ師ㄕ

張ㄓㄤ伯ㄅㄛˊ伯ㄅㄛˊ

王ㄨㄤˊ芸ㄩㄣˊ

李ㄌㄧˇ立ㄌㄧˋ

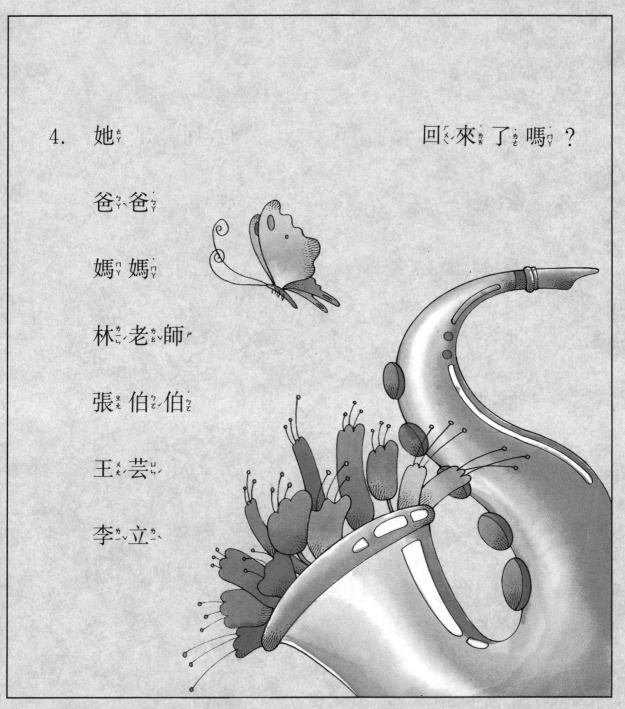

Ⅲ 句型練習

(Pattern Practice)

5.　她（ㄊㄚ）　　　　　　　　也（一ㄝˇ）回（ㄏㄨㄟˊ）來（ㄌㄞˊ）了（ㄌㄜ˙）。

　　爸（ㄅㄚˋ）爸（ㄅㄚ˙）

　　媽（ㄇㄚ）媽（ㄇㄚ˙）

　　哥（ㄍㄜ）哥（ㄍㄜ˙）

　　姐（ㄐㄧㄝˇ）姐（ㄐㄧㄝ˙）

　　弟（ㄉㄧˋ）弟（ㄉㄧ˙）

　　妹（ㄇㄟˋ）妹（ㄇㄟ˙）

6. 她_{ㄊㄚ} 在_{ㄗㄞˋ} 那_{ㄋㄚˇ} 兒_ㄦ ？

爸_{ㄅㄚˋ}爸_{ㄅㄚ˙}

媽_{ㄇㄚ}媽_{ㄇㄚ˙}

哥_{ㄍㄜ}哥_{ㄍㄜ˙}

姐_{ㄐㄧㄝˇ}姐_{ㄐㄧㄝ˙}

弟_{ㄉㄧˋ}弟_{ㄉㄧ˙}

妹_{ㄇㄟˋ}妹_{ㄇㄟ˙}

Ⅳ英　譯

(English Translation)

Part　1：

王ㄨㄤˊ　芸ㄩㄣˊ
Good morning, Dad.
Good morning, Mom.

爸ㄅㄚˋ　媽ㄇㄚ
Good morning！Shiau Yun.

(Getting dressed and having breakfast)

王ㄨㄤˊ　芸ㄩㄣˊ
Hurry up！　Gege.
Hurry up！　Jiejie.

哥ㄍㄜ　哥ㄍㄜ
The school bus has arrived, hasn't it？

王ㄨㄤˊ　芸ㄩㄣˊ
Yes, it has arrived.

哥ㄍㄜ　哥ㄍㄜ
Bye, Dad. Bye, Mom.

姐ㄐㄧˇ 姐ㄐㄧㄝ˙	Bye, Dad.　Bye, Mom.
王ㄨㄤˊ 芸ㄩㄣˊ	Bye, Dad. Bye, Mom.
李ㄌㄧˇ 立ㄌㄧˋ	Mom！　I'm back.　Has Dad come home yet？
媽ㄇㄚ 媽ㄇㄚ˙	Yes, he has.
李ㄌㄧˇ 立ㄌㄧˋ	How about my younger sister？
媽ㄇㄚ 媽ㄇㄚ˙	She's come home too.
李ㄌㄧˇ 立ㄌㄧˋ	Where is she？
媽ㄇㄚ 媽ㄇㄚ˙	In the back yard

IV 英 譯

(English Translation)

李立 How about my younger brother?

媽媽 He's over at Uncle Jang's.

第三課

我的朋友

My Friend

I 對 話

（ Dialogue ）

第 一 部	Part 1
李立	媽，她是我的朋友
媽媽	你叫什麼名字？
王芸	我叫王芸。李媽媽好！
媽媽	你好，王芸。請坐！
王芸	謝謝！
李立	這是我弟弟，他叫李德。
王芸	你好，李德。
李德	你好，王姐姐。
李立	這是我妹妹，她叫李欣欣。

王ㄨㄤˊ　芸ㄩㄣˊ　　你ㄋㄧˇ好ㄏㄠˇ，李ㄌㄧˇ欣ㄒㄧㄣ欣ㄒㄧㄣ。

李ㄌㄧˇ欣ㄒㄧㄣ欣ㄒㄧㄣ　你ㄋㄧˇ好ㄏㄠˇ，王ㄨㄤˊ姐ㄐㄧㄝˇ姐ㄐㄧㄝ。你ㄋㄧˇ要ㄧㄠˋ喝ㄏㄜ

　　　　　　可ㄎㄜˇ樂ㄌㄜˋ嗎ㄇㄚ？

王ㄨㄤˊ　芸ㄩㄣˊ　　好ㄏㄠˇ啊ㄚ！

王ㄨㄤˊ　芸ㄩㄣˊ　　謝ㄒㄧㄝˋ謝ㄒㄧㄝ你ㄋㄧˇ！

李ㄌㄧˇ欣ㄒㄧㄣ欣ㄒㄧㄣ　不ㄅㄨˋ客ㄎㄜˋ氣ㄑㄧˋ！

Ⅰ 對 話

(Dialogue)

第 二 部	Part 2
李立	誰啊？
李德	一定是林一平，我去看看。
李德	嗨！一平。
林一平	嗨！李德
李德	媽，這是我的朋友林一平。
林一平	李媽媽好！
媽媽	你好，一平。請坐！
林一平	謝謝！

Ⅱ 生字生詞

(Vocabulary & Expressions)

1. 朋友（友） friend

2. 請 please

3. 坐 sit

4. 謝謝 thanks

5. 這 this

6. 他 he, him

7. 德 (a person's given name)

8. 欣欣 (a person's given name)

9. 要 want

10. 喝 drink

11. 可樂 cola

12. 不客氣 You're welcome.

13. 誰 who

14. 一定 It must be...

15. 一平 (a person's given name)

16. 去 go

17. 看看 see ; look

18. 嗨 hi

Ⅲ 句型練習

(Pattern Practice)

1. 她是 我的 朋友。

   她是 我的 妹妹。

   他是 我的 弟弟。

   他是 我的 爸爸。

   這是 我的 媽媽。

   這是 他的 哥哥。

2.

可ㄎㄜˇ 樂ㄌㄜˋ

喝ㄏㄜ 可ㄎㄜˇ 樂ㄌㄜˋ

要ㄠˋ 喝ㄏㄜ 可ㄎㄜˇ 樂ㄌㄜˋ

要ㄠˋ 喝ㄏㄜ 可ㄎㄜˇ 樂ㄌㄜˋ 嗎ㄇㄚˇ？

你ㄋㄧˇ 要ㄠˋ 喝ㄏㄜ 可ㄎㄜˇ 樂ㄌㄜˋ 嗎ㄇㄚˇ？

媽ㄇㄚ 媽ㄇㄚˇ 要ㄠˋ 喝ㄏㄜ 可ㄎㄜˇ 樂ㄌㄜˋ 嗎ㄇㄚˇ？

Ⅲ 句型練習

(Pattern Practice)

3. 　　　　　　　是ㄕˋ他ㄊㄚ

　　　　一ㄧˊ定ㄉㄧㄥˋ是ㄕˋ他ㄊㄚ

　　　一ㄧˊ定ㄉㄧㄥˋ是ㄕˋ他ㄊㄚ姐ㄐㄧㄝˇ姐ㄐㄧㄝ

　　　一ㄧˊ定ㄉㄧㄥˋ是ㄕˋ林ㄌㄧㄣˊ一ㄧ平ㄆㄧㄥˊ

4. 　　　　　　　看ㄎㄢˋ看ㄎㄢ

　　　　　去ㄑㄩˋ看ㄎㄢˋ看ㄎㄢ

　　　　我ㄨㄛˇ去ㄑㄩˋ看ㄎㄢˋ看ㄎㄢ

　　　請ㄑㄧㄥˇ你ㄋㄧˇ去ㄑㄩˋ看ㄎㄢˋ看ㄎㄢ

Ⅳ英 譯

（ English Translation ）

Part　1：

李ㄌㄧˇ　立ㄌㄧˋ　　Mom, this is my friend.

媽ㄇㄚ　媽ㄇㄚ　　What's your name？

王ㄨㄤˊ　芸ㄩㄣˊ　　My name is 王ㄨㄤˊ　芸ㄩㄣˊ.

　　　　　　　　How do you do, Mrs. 李ㄌㄧˇ？

媽ㄇㄚ　媽ㄇㄚ　　Good！How are you？ 王ㄨㄤˊ　芸ㄩㄣˊ

　　　　　　　　Please, have a seat.

王ㄨㄤˊ　芸ㄩㄣˊ　　Thank you.

李ㄌㄧˇ　立ㄌㄧˋ　　This is my younger brother.

　　　　　　　　His name is 李ㄌㄧˇ　德ㄉㄜˊ.

Ⅳ 英 譯

(English Translation)

王ㄨㄤˊ 芸ㄩㄣˊ | How are you ， 李ㄌㄧˇ 德ㄉㄜˊ .
Lǐ　　Dé

李ㄌㄧˇ 德ㄉㄜˊ | Good ！ How are you ， Sister 王ㄨㄤˊ .
Wáng

李ㄌㄧˇ 立ㄌㄧˋ | This is my younger sister.

Her name is 李ㄌㄧˇ欣ㄒㄧㄣ欣ㄒㄧㄣ .
Lǐ Shin—shin

王ㄨㄤˊ 芸ㄩㄣˊ | How are you ？ 李ㄌㄧˇ欣ㄒㄧㄣ欣ㄒㄧㄣ .
Lǐ Shin—shin

李ㄌㄧˇ欣ㄒㄧㄣ欣ㄒㄧㄣ | Fine. How are you ， Sister 王ㄨㄤˊ .
Wáng

Would you like some cola ？

王ㄨㄤˊ 芸ㄩㄣˊ | Yes, please.

王ㄨㄤˊ 芸ㄩㄣˊ | Thank you ！

李ㄌㄧˇ欣ㄒㄧㄣ欣ㄒㄧㄣ | You're welcome.

Part 2：

（Ding Dong！The door bell rings.）

李ㄌㄧˇ　立ㄌㄧˋ　　Who is it？

李ㄌㄧˇ　德ㄉㄜˊ　　It must be 林ㄌㄧㄣˊ一ㄧ平ㄆㄧㄥˊ.　I'll go take a look.

李ㄌㄧˇ　德ㄉㄜˊ　　Hi！一ㄧ平ㄆㄧㄥˊ.

林ㄌㄧㄣˊ一ㄧ平ㄆㄧㄥˊ　　Hi！李ㄌㄧˇ德ㄉㄜˊ.

李ㄌㄧˇ　德ㄉㄜˊ　　Mom, this is my friend 林ㄌㄧㄣˊ一ㄧ平ㄆㄧㄥˊ.

林ㄌㄧㄣˊ一ㄧ平ㄆㄧㄥˊ　　How are you ，　Mrs. 李ㄌㄧˇ.

Ⅳ英 譯

(English Translation)

媽ㄇㄚ 媽ㄇㄚ	Good！ How are you？ 一ㄧ平ㄆㄥ.
	Have a seat, please.
林ㄌㄧㄣ一ㄧ平ㄆㄥ	Thanks.

第四課

カ丶 ム丶 ちˋ

數 一 數

アˇ ㄧ丶 アˇ
ㄕㄨˇ ㄕㄨˇ

Let's Count.

Ⅰ對 話

（ Dialogue ）

第　一　部	Part　1
李欣欣	王姐姐，你有弟弟，妹妹嗎？
王　芸	沒有。我有哥哥，姐姐。
李欣欣	幾個哥哥？幾個姐姐？
王　芸	一個哥哥，一個姐姐。
李欣欣	林一平，你呢？
林一平	我有兩個妹妹。

第二部	Part 2
李立	你們要不要吃點兒點心？
李欣欣	好啊！
李立	有爆米花，巧克力糖 和餅乾。
李欣欣	有沒有冰淇淋？
李立	有。
李立	我們有很多爆米花。
王芸	有幾盒？
李立	有六盒。

Ⅰ對　話

（ Dialogue ）

李德	巧克力糖呢？
李立	有八盒。
李欣欣	有多少餅乾？
李立	我不知道，請你數數看吧！
李欣欣	一，二，三，四，五，六，七，八，九，十 啊！有十盒。

Ⅱ 生字生詞

（ Vocabulary & Expressions ）

1. 數ㄕㄨˇ   to count

2. 數ㄕㄨˇ 一一 數ㄕㄨˇ （ Let's ） count

3. 有ㄧㄡˇ   has, have, had

4. 沒ㄇㄟˊ有ㄧㄡˇ   don't have
                 doesn't have

5. 幾ㄐㄧˇ   how many

6. 個ㄍㄜˋ   (measure word)

7. 一ㄧ   one

8. 兩ㄌㄧㄤˇ   two

9. 你ㄋㄧˇ們ㄇㄣ˙   you （ pl. ）

10. 要ㄧㄠˋ不ㄅㄨˋ要ㄧㄠˋ （ Do you ） want
                 it or not, would
                 you like

11. 吃ㄔ   eat

12. 點ㄉㄧㄢˇ心ㄒㄧㄣ   snack

13. 爆ㄅㄠˋ米ㄇㄧˇ花ㄏㄨㄚ popcorn

14. 巧ㄑㄧㄠˇ克ㄎㄜˋ力ㄌㄧˋ糖ㄊㄤˊ chocolate

15. 和ㄏㄢˋ（ㄏㄜˊ）   and

16. 餅ㄅㄧㄥˇ乾ㄍㄢ   cookie

17. 有ㄧㄡˇ沒ㄇㄟˊ有ㄧㄡˇ has （ have ） or
                 has （ have ）
                 not

Ⅱ 生字生詞

(Vocabulary & Expressions)

18. 冰淇淋 ice cream

19. 我們 we

20. 很多 many

21. 盒 box

22. 六 six

23. 八 eight

24. 多少（少）how many

25. 不（不）don't, doesn't

26. 知道（道）know

27. 數數看（Let's）count

28. 吧 (exclamation word)

29. 二 two

30. 三 three

31. 四 four

32. 五 five

33. 七 seven

34. 九 nine

35. 十 ten

III 句型練習

（ Pattern Practice ）

1.　你ˇ　　　有ˇ　　弟ㄉ一ˋ弟ㄉ一　　嗎ㄇㄚ？

　　你ˇ　　　有ˇ　　妹ㄇㄟˋ妹ㄇㄟ　　嗎ㄇㄚ？

　　他ㄊㄚ　　有ˇ　　姐ㄐㄧㄝˇ姐ㄐㄧㄝ　　嗎ㄇㄚ？

　　他ㄊㄚ們ㄇㄣ　有ˇ　　哥ㄍㄜ哥ㄍㄜ　　嗎ㄇㄚ？

2.　我ㄨㄛˇ　　　沒ㄇㄟˊ有ˇ　哥ㄍㄜ哥ㄍㄜ。

　　你ˇ　　　　沒ㄇㄟˊ有ˇ　姐ㄐㄧㄝˇ姐ㄐㄧㄝ。

　　他ㄊㄚ　　　沒ㄇㄟˊ有ˇ　妹ㄇㄟˋ妹ㄇㄟ。

　　你ˇ們ㄇㄣ　　沒ㄇㄟˊ有ˇ　弟ㄉㄧˋ弟ㄉㄧ。

49

Ⅲ 句型練習

（ Pattern Practice ）

3. 你ㄋㄧˇ　　有ㄧㄡˇ幾ㄐㄧˇ個ㄍㄜˋ　哥ㄍㄜ哥ㄍㄜ˙ ？

　　他ㄊㄚ　　有ㄧㄡˇ幾ㄐㄧˇ個ㄍㄜˋ　姐ㄐㄧㄝˇ姐ㄐㄧㄝ˙ ？

　　她ㄊㄚ　　有ㄧㄡˇ幾ㄐㄧˇ個ㄍㄜˋ　弟ㄉㄧˋ弟ㄉㄧ˙ ？

　　他ㄊㄚ們ㄇㄣ˙　有ㄧㄡˇ幾ㄐㄧˇ個ㄍㄜˋ　妹ㄇㄟˋ妹ㄇㄟ˙ ？

4. 我ㄨㄛˇ　　有ㄧㄡˇ　一ㄧ個ㄍㄜˋ　哥ㄍㄜ哥ㄍㄜ˙ 。

　　他ㄊㄚ　　有ㄧㄡˇ　兩ㄌㄧㄤˇ個ㄍㄜˋ　姐ㄐㄧㄝˇ姐ㄐㄧㄝ˙ 。

　　你ㄋㄧˇ　　有ㄧㄡˇ　三ㄙㄢ個ㄍㄜˋ　妹ㄇㄟˋ妹ㄇㄟ˙ 。

　　我ㄨㄛˇ們ㄇㄣ˙　有ㄧㄡˇ　四ㄙˋ個ㄍㄜˋ　弟ㄉㄧˋ弟ㄉㄧ˙ 。

5. 你們　要不要　吃點兒　點心？

　　你　　要不要　喝點兒　可樂？

　　他　　要不要　吃點兒　爆米花？

　　她　　要不要　吃點兒　巧克力糖？

　　他們　要不要　吃點兒　餅乾？

　　爸爸　要不要　吃點兒　冰淇淋？

6. 你　　有沒有　冰淇淋？

　　你　　有沒有　哥哥？

　　她　　有沒有　姐姐？

　　你們　有沒有　妹妹？

51

Ⅲ 句型練習

(Pattern Practice)

7.　我ㄨㄛˇ們ㄇㄣ·　有ㄧㄡˇ　很ㄏㄣˇ多ㄉㄨㄛ　爆ㄅㄠˋ米ㄇㄧˇ花ㄏㄨㄚ。

　　你ㄋㄧˇ們ㄇㄣ·　有ㄧㄡˇ　很ㄏㄣˇ多ㄉㄨㄛ　餅ㄅㄧㄥˇ乾ㄍㄢ。

　　他ㄊㄚ們ㄇㄣ·　有ㄧㄡˇ　六ㄌㄧㄡˋ盒ㄏㄜˊ　巧ㄑㄧㄠˇ克ㄎㄜˋ力ㄌㄧˋ糖ㄊㄤ。

　　他ㄊㄚ　　有ㄧㄡˇ　三ㄙㄢ個ㄍㄜˋ　姐ㄐㄧㄝˇ姐ㄐㄧㄝ·。

8.　有ㄧㄡˇ多ㄉㄨㄛ少ㄕㄠˇ　　　　　餅ㄅㄧㄥˇ乾ㄍㄢ？

　　有ㄧㄡˇ多ㄉㄨㄛ少ㄕㄠˇ　　　　　冰ㄅㄧㄥ淇ㄑㄧˊ淋ㄌㄧㄣˊ？

　　有ㄧㄡˇ多ㄉㄨㄛ少ㄕㄠˇ　　　　　巧ㄑㄧㄠˇ克ㄎㄜˋ力ㄌㄧˋ糖ㄊㄤ？

Ⅳ英 譯

(English Translation)

Part 1：

李ㄌㄧˇ欣ㄒㄧㄣ欣ㄒㄧㄣ   Wang Jiejie, do you have any younger brothers or sisters？

王ㄨㄤˊ 芸ㄩㄣˊ   No.   I have older brothers and sisters.

李ㄌㄧˇ欣ㄒㄧㄣ欣ㄒㄧㄣ   How many？

王ㄨㄤˊ 芸ㄩㄣˊ   An older brother and an older sister.

李ㄌㄧˇ欣ㄒㄧㄣ欣ㄒㄧㄣ   Lin Yi—ping, what about you？

林ㄌㄧㄣˊ一一平ㄆㄧㄥˊ   I have two younger sisters.

53

Ⅳ 英 譯

(English Translation)

Part 2 ：

李立	Would you like some snacks ？
李欣欣	Yes, please.
李立	We have some popcorn, chocolate, and cookies.
李欣欣	Do we have any ice cream ？
李立	Yes.
李立	We have lots of popcorn.
王芸	How many boxes ？

54

李立_{ㄌㄧˇ ㄌㄧˋ}		Six boxes.
李德_{ㄌㄧˇ ㄉㄜˊ}		And chocolate ?
李立_{ㄌㄧˇ ㄌㄧˋ}		Eight boxes.
李欣欣_{ㄌㄧˇ ㄒㄧㄣ ㄒㄧㄣ}		How many cookies do we have ?
李立_{ㄌㄧˇ ㄌㄧˋ}		I don't know.　Would you please count them ?
李欣欣_{ㄌㄧˇ ㄒㄧㄣ ㄒㄧㄣ}		One, two, three, four, five, six, seven, eight, nine, ten. Oh！ Ten boxes.

生字生詞索引 Index

國語注音符號	生 字 生 詞 Vocabulary & Expressions	英　　　　　　　　　　　　譯 English Translation	課 次 及 頁 次 Lesson Page
ㄅ			
ㄅㄚ	八	eight	4-48
	爸爸	Dad	2-20
	吧	(exclamation word)	4-48
ㄅㄛ	伯伯	uncle	1-6
ㄅㄠ	爆米花	popcorn	4-47
ㄅㄧㄥ	冰淇淋	ice cream	4-48
	餅乾	cookie	4-47
ㄅㄨ	不客氣	You're welcome	3-35
	不，不，不	not(i. e. the negative)	2-20
ㄆ			
ㄆㄥ	朋友	friend	3-35
ㄇ			
ㄇㄚ	媽媽	Mon	2-20
	嗎	(question word)	2-21
ㄇㄟ	沒有	don't have, doesn't have	4-47

56

	妹ㄇㄟ 妹ㄇㄟ	younger sister	2-21
ㄇㄥ	名ㄇㄥ 字ㄗ	name	1-5
ㄅ			
ㄅㄜ	德ㄉㄜ	(a person's given name)	3-35
	的ㄉㄜ	(possessive word)	2-20
ㄅㄧ	弟ㄉㄧ 弟ㄉㄧ	younger brother	2-21
ㄅㄢ	點ㄉㄧㄢ 心ㄒㄧㄣ	snack	4-47
ㄅㄨㄛ	多ㄉㄨㄛ 少ㄕㄠ	how many	4-48
ㄅㄨㄟ	對ㄉㄨㄟ	yes, right	2-20
	對ㄉㄨㄟ 了ㄌㄜ	right, correct	1-6
ㄊ			
ㄊㄚ	他ㄊㄚ	he, him	3-35
	她ㄊㄚ	she, her	2-21
ㄋ			
ㄋㄚ	那ㄋㄚ 兒ㄦ	where	2-21
ㄋㄜ	呢ㄋㄜ	(question word)	2-21
ㄋㄧ	你ㄋㄧ	you(singular)	1-5
	你ㄋㄧ 們ㄇㄣ	you(pl.)	4-47

57

生字生詞索引	Index

國語 注音 符號	生 字 生 詞 Vocabulary & Expressions	英　　　　　　　　　　　　譯 English Translation	課 次 及 頁 　 次 Lesson Page
	3		
	您ㄋㄧㄣ好ㄏㄠ	How are you ?	1-5
ㄋㄧㄣ	您ㄋㄧㄣ	you;(showing politeness, respect and honor)	1-5
	ㄌ		
ㄌㄜ	了ㄌㄜ	verb suffix or sentence suffix, indicating completion of an action.	2-20
ㄌㄞ	來ㄌㄞ	come	2-20
ㄌㄠ	老ㄌㄠ師ㄕ	teacher	1-5
ㄌㄧ	李ㄌㄧ	(a family name)	1-5
	立ㄌㄧ	(a given name)	1-5
ㄌㄡ	六ㄌㄡ	six	4-48
ㄌㄧㄣ	林ㄌㄧㄣ	(a family name)	1-5
ㄌㄧㄤ	兩ㄌㄧㄤ	two	4-47
	ㄍ		

58

ㄍㄜ	哥ㄍㄜ哥ㄍㄜ	older brother	2-20
	個ㄍㄜ	(measure word)	4-47
ㄍㄨㄟ	貴ㄍㄨㄟ姓ㄒㄧㄥ	What's your (nonorable) family name?	1-5
ㄎ			
ㄎㄜ	可ㄎㄜ樂ㄌㄜ	cola	3-35
ㄎㄢ	看ㄎㄢ看ㄎㄢ	see, look	3-35
ㄎㄨㄞ	快ㄎㄨㄞ	Hurry up!	2-20
ㄏ			
ㄏㄜ	喝ㄏㄜ	drink	3-35
	盒ㄏㄜ	box	4-48
ㄏㄞ	嗨ㄏㄞ	Hi!	3-35
ㄏㄡ	後ㄏㄡ院ㄩㄢ兒ㄦ	back yard	2-21
ㄏㄢ	和ㄏㄢ	and	4-47
ㄏㄣ	很ㄏㄣ多ㄉㄨㄛ	many	4-48
ㄏㄨㄟ	回ㄏㄨㄟ來ㄌㄞ	come back, return	2-21
ㄐ			
ㄐㄧ	幾ㄐㄧ	how many	4-47

59

生字生詞索引	Index

國語 注音 符號	生　字　生　詞 Vocabulary & Expressions	英　　　　　　　　　　　　譯 English Translation	課　次　及 頁　　　次 Lesson Page
ㄐ			
ㄐㄚ	家ㄐㄚ	home	2-20
ㄐㄝ	姐ㄐㄝ姐ㄐㄝ	older sister	2-20
ㄐㄠ	叫ㄐㄠ	My name is … I'm	1-5
ㄐㄡ	九ㄐㄡ	nine	4-48
ㄑ			
ㄑㄧ	七ㄑㄧ	seven	4-48
ㄑㄠ	巧ㄑㄠ克ㄎㄜ力ㄌㄧ糖ㄊㄤ	chocolate	4-47
ㄑㄥ	請ㄑㄥ	please	3-35
	請ㄑㄥ問ㄨㄣ	Excuse me, but (My I ask you …… ？)	1-6
ㄑㄩ	去ㄑㄩ	go	3-35
ㄏ			
ㄒㄝ	謝ㄒㄝ謝ㄒㄝ	thanks	3-35
ㄒㄠ	小ㄒㄠ	little	2-20
	校ㄒㄠ車ㄔㄜ	school bus	2-20

ㄒㄧㄣ	欣ㄒㄧㄣ 欣ㄒㄧㄣ	(a person's given name)	3-35
ㄒㄧㄥ	姓ㄒㄧㄥ	family name, last name	1-5
ㄓ			
ㄓ	知ㄓ 道ㄉㄠ	know	4-48
ㄓㄜ	這ㄓㄜ	this	3-35
ㄓㄤ	張ㄓㄤ	(a family name)	1-6
ㄔ			
ㄔ	吃ㄔ	eat	4-47
ㄕ			
ㄕ	十ㄕ	ten	4-48
	是ㄕ	to be (am, is, are, was, were)	1-6
ㄕㄜ	什ㄕㄜ 麼ㄇㄜ	what	1-5
ㄕㄟ	誰ㄕㄟ	who	3-35
ㄕㄨ	數ㄕㄨ 數ㄕㄨ 看ㄎㄢ	(Let's) count	4-48
	數ㄕㄨ	to count	4-47
	數ㄕㄨ 一一 數ㄕㄨ	(Let's) count	4-47
ㄗ			
ㄗㄞ	在ㄗㄞ	to be(in a location)	2-21

生字生詞索引 Index

國語注音符號	生 字 生 詞 Vocabulary & Expressions	英　　　　　　　　　　　　　　　　　　　　譯 English Translation	課 次 及 頁 次 Lesson Page
ㄗ			
	再ㄗㄞ見ㄐㄧㄢ	See you! Good-bye!	1-6
ㄗㄠ	早ㄗㄠ	Good morning!	1-5
ㄗㄨㄛ	坐ㄗㄨㄛ	sit	3-35
ㄙ			
ㄙ	四ㄙ	four	4-48
ㄙㄢ	三ㄙㄢ	three	4-48
ㄚ			
ㄚ	啊ㄚ	(exclamation)Ah!	2-20
ㄛ			
ㄛ	喔ㄛ	(exclamation)Oh!	1-5
ㄦ			
ㄦ	二ㄦ	two	4-48
ㄧ			
ㄧ	一ㄧ	one	4-47
	一ㄧ平ㄆㄥ	(a person's given name)	3-35

	一ˊ定ㄉㄧㄥˋ	It must be ……	3-35
	（一ˊ）點ㄉㄧㄢˇ兒ㄦ	a little	2-20
一ㄝ	也ㄧㄝˇ	also, too	2-21
一ㄠ	要ㄧㄠˋ	want	3-35
	要ㄧㄠˋ不ㄅㄨˋ要ㄧㄠˋ	(Do you) want it or not, would you like ……	4-47
一ㄡ	有ㄧㄡˇ	has, have, had	4-47
	有ㄧㄡˇ沒ㄇㄟˊ有ㄧㄡˇ	has (have) or has (have) not	4-47
ㄨ			
ㄨ	五ㄨˇ	five	4-48
ㄨㄛ	我ㄨㄛˇ	I, me	1-5
	我ㄨㄛˇ們ㄇㄣ	we	4-48
	我ㄨㄛˇ的ㄉㄜ	my	2-20
ㄨㄤ	王ㄨㄤˊ	(a family name)	1-5
ㄩ			
ㄩㄣ	芸ㄩㄣˊ	(a given name)	1-5

這是我的家

天地 曲

這 是 我 的 家 ， 我 們 都 愛 他 ，

池 裡 養 著 魚 ， 園 裡 種 著 花 ，

園 外 有 田 地 ， 種 豆 又 種 瓜 。

64

小鬧鐘

上官亮　詞
范宇文　曲

ㄉㄜ ㄉㄧㄥ ㄉㄧㄥ ㄉㄧㄥ ㄉㄧㄥ　ㄉㄧㄥ ㄉㄧㄥ ㄉㄧㄥ ！ 我是一個我是一個小鬧鐘，

不管白天和晚上，　隨時為您 ㄉㄜ ㄉㄧㄥ ㄉㄧㄥ ！

不管兵與工商農，　隨時為您 催好夢。

不管春夏和秋冬，　努力工作 莫放鬆。

媽媽的眼睛

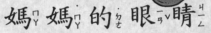

美麗的 美麗的 天空裡，
媽媽的 眼睛 我最喜愛，

出來了 光亮的 小星星，
常常的 希望我 做個好小孩，

好像是 我媽媽 慈愛的眼睛。
媽媽的 眼睛 我最喜愛。

兒童華語課本（一）中英文版

主　　編：王孫元平、何景賢、宋靜如、馬昭華、葉德明

出版機關：中華民國僑務委員會

地址：台北市徐州路五號十六樓

電話：(02)3343-2600

網址：http://www.ocac.gov.tw

出版年月：中華民國八十一年十二月初版

版（刷次）：中華民國九十二年四月初版七刷

定　　價：新台幣八十元

展 售 處：三民書局（台北市重慶南路一段61號，電話：02-23617511）

國家書坊台視總店（台北市八德路三段10號，電話：02-25781515）

五南文化廣場（台中市中山路2號，電話：04-2260330）

新進圖書廣場（彰化市光復路177號，電話：04-7252792）

青年書局（高雄市青年一路141號，電話：07-3324910）

承　　印：文芳印刷事務有限公司

GPN：011099870136

ISBN：957-02-1648-4